INSIDE MAGIC

STAND-UP MAGIC AND OPTICAL ILLUSIONS

Nicholas Einhorn

rosen publishing's
rosen
central

New York

This edition published in 2011 by:

The Rosen Publishing Group, Inc.
29 East 21st Street
New York, NY 10010

Library of Congress Cataloging-in-Publication Data

Einhorn, Nicholas.
Stand-up magic and optical illusions / Nicholas Einhorn.
   p. cm.—(Inside magic)
Includes bibliographical references and index.
ISBN 978-1-4358-9452-5 (library binding)
1. Magic tricks—Juvenile literature. 2. Optical illusions—Juvenile literature. I. Title.
GV1548.E334 2011
793.8—dc22

2010010113

Manufactured in the United States of America

CPSIA Compliance Information: Batch #S10YA: For further information, contact Rosen Publishing, New York, New York, at 1-800-237-9932.

Copyright in design, text and images © 2007, 2009 Anness Publishing Limited, U.K. Previously published as part of a larger volume: *Magical Illusions, Conjuring Tricks, Amazing Puzzles & Stunning Stunts.*

Photography by Paul Bricknell © Anness

CONTENTS

INTRODUCTION

The kind of performance described by the all-encompassing term "stand-up magic" could also be described as "cabaret magic," "parlor magic," or even "stage magic." Performances of this type may take place on a stage, a dance floor, in a hall, perhaps even in someone's living room, but the defining characteristic of all tricks in this genre is that they are suitable for a large audience. Often these performances make use of large props, and sometimes members of the audience may be required to assist with the tricks. The key to choosing material for a stand-up magic act is visibility. What you are doing must be highly visible to everyone watching.

In this book, you'll find tricks that you can do in front of a bigger audience. While many of these would also work for a smaller crowd, they are similar in style to the tricks performed by magicians as part of a stage show. Often this means that you will use larger props, but it does not mean they will cost you a lot of money. You will find that many of the items required can either be found at home or purchased inexpensively from a local store.

This book contains more than just magic tricks, and there is a good reason for this. Besides knowing the secrets, a good magician needs to appreciate how our minds can play tricks on us, and the section on optical illusions shows how we can be made to see things in different ways.

This book contains a variety of optical illusions, including two-dimensional images that will confuse your brain, and those that require your input to make the illusions happen. Those that can be performed make ideal party tricks, or can be incorporated into a stand-up show to add an extra dimension. One thing is certain: As you proceed through this book, you'll find it hard to believe your eyes!

Production Tube

A roll of card stock, which is opened and shown to be empty, is rolled back into a tube and used to produce silk handkerchiefs from thin air. You can use this simple prop to make anything that fits inside the tube appear or disappear.

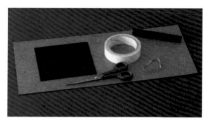

1. To make the tube you will need a piece of red card stock approximately 12 x 24 in (30 x 60 cm), a piece of black cardstock approximately 4 x 6 in (10 x 15 cm), some double-sided adhesive tape, a pair of scissors, a rubber band and a pen.

2. Fold the red card in half across its width, making a sharp crease.

3. Attach a piece of double-sided tape to one of the shorter sides of the black card. Starting from the opposite side, roll the card into a tube and secure it neatly with the tape.

4. With the red card still folded in half, roll it up tightly from the folded edge.

5. Secure the tube with a rubber band and leave overnight, so that when the band is removed the tube holds its shape.

6. Use a piece of double-sided tape to secure the black tube to the center of the red card along the crease, as shown. This is a secret compartment that will never be seen by the spectators.

7. Mark a black dot on the red card, on the edge of the section with the secret compartment. Make sure the tube is oriented as shown here before you mark it.

8. Place the rubber band around the tube to hold it in place as you insert three colored silks, one at a time, into the secret compartment.

9. Twist the ends of the silks together as they go into the tube. This will make it easier to remove them during the performance.

10. Once you have put all three silks inside the secret compartment remove the band, and you are ready to perform the trick.

11. Begin by showing the tube of red card stock to the audience.

12. Pull the tube open, making sure that your right hand holds the edge with the black dot you made earlier.

Secret View

13. The view from above shows exactly what is happening.

14. When the tube is fully unrolled, it will look like a plain piece of card stock.

15. The secret compartment is hidden on the back.

16. Roll the card back up into a loose tube again.

17. Reach in and remove the first of the silk handkerchiefs.

18. Then remove the other silks and once again open the tube to show the audience that it is empty.

Blended Silks (version 1)

Four separate silks are pushed into an empty card tube. They come out joined together as one blended square. This is another trick you can do using the production tube with the secret compartment that is described on page 5.

1. Using double-sided adhesive tape, carefully join the edges of four silks to make a large square. Insert this special silk into the secret compartment of your production tube.

2. When you perform the trick, have four separate silks in the same four colors displayed in a glass and show the tube empty as described previously.

3. Pick up the separate silks one at a time, and insert them into the secret compartment on top of the prepared silk.

4. Slowly pull out the blended silk from the bottom of the tube.

5. Open it up to show that the four different colored silks have joined together as one.

6. Finish by opening the tube to show it empty. The separate silks are safely hidden in the secret compartment.

Magic Photo Album

A photograph album is seen to be completely empty, only to be shown filled with pictures a few seconds later. This clever trick utilizes a principle called "short and long," which can be put to all sorts of uses in stand-up magic and card tricks.

1. Slice the edge off every other page in a photograph album. The first page should be cut short, the next left long, the next cut short, and so on.

2. Insert photographs into every other pair of pages, starting with pages 2 and 3, then 6 and 7, and so on.

3. Hold up the prepared album and explain to the spectators that you have some holiday snapshots you would like to share with them.

4. If you open the album and flip through the pages from the back to the front, every page will appear blank. This is because you made every other page short and therefore the pages fall in pairs. The photographs are all located on the pages that are not seen.

5. Explain that the album is empty, but that you will use your magic to fill it up. Make a magical gesture and then open the album once again, but this time flip through the pages from the front to the back. Once again the pages will fall in pairs, but now the blank pages will remain hidden and the album will appear to be full of pictures.

Needles Through Balloon

A cardboard tube is shown empty. A long modeling balloon is inflated inside the tube so that both ends can be seen. Several long needles or skewers are pushed through the center of the tube at all angles but the balloon does not burst. The needles are removed and the balloon is popped to finish the routine. There is more than one way of performing this trick; two of them are explained below.

1. You will need a modeling balloon, a piece of card stock, a ruler, a pencil, a craft knife, adhesive tape, skewers, and some adhesive glue.

2. Divide the card into five equal sections using a ruler so that you can create a square-section tube. (The size of this tube will depend on the size of the balloon you are using.) Fold the card.

3. Apply glue to the inside of the last section and glue it over the first section to create the tube.

4. The finished card tube should look like this, and should be secure.

5. Carefully using a craft knife, make several star-shaped cuts in the card in different locations. Look at steps 10 and 11 to see the exact locations.

6. You can decorate your tube with a piece of colored tape, if you wish.

Secret View

7. In performance, show the balloon and the tube.

8. Blow up the balloon through the tube and knot the end. The balloon should fit snugly, but not too tightly, inside the tube.

9. Secretly twist the balloon so that the twist is hidden inside the tube.

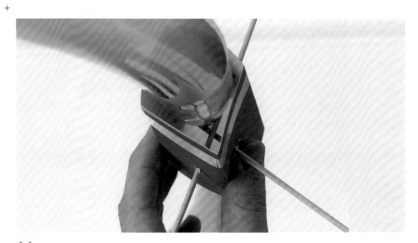

10. You can now push a skewer through one of the star-shaped cuts in the tube and out the other side. The twist in the balloon provides the space needed by the skewer.

11. Push another skewer in at a different angle. It looks as though it is impossible to do this without bursting the balloon. This secret view shows how the skewers go around the balloon inside the tube.

Secret View

12. Modeling balloons are naturally flexible, so instead of twisting the balloon inside the tube (step 10) you can simply use the skewers to push it out of the way as they pass through the tube. This secret view shows how the skewer avoids the balloon as it enters. Notice how the balloon is pushed to one side.

13. The effect is identical. You can use either method – both work perfectly.

Vanishing Glass of Liquid

A glass is filled with liquid from a pitcher. The glass is covered with a handkerchief and tossed in the air, and both the glass and the liquid vanish instantly. This stunning trick requires two gimmicks to be made. The first is a special cloth, made from two identical layers stitched or glued together, with a disc of cardboard in the middle. When held from above the illusion of a glass under the cloth is perfect. The second gimmick is a specially prepared pitcher, which only takes a few minutes to modify.

1. Trace the glass you will be using on a piece of thick cardboard and cut out this circle.

2. Stick the cardboard disc to the center of a small square of cloth. Then stick an identical cloth on top, sandwiching the disc in the middle.

3. The pitcher must be opaque and should be big enough to hide the glass inside it. Line the inside of the pitcher with a bubble wrap bag. Leave the section closest to the spout open.

Secret View

4. This is what the prepared pitcher looks like when you have lined it.

5. To prepare, pour some liquid into the pitcher between the open portion of the bubble wrap and the side of the pitcher.

6. Have the cloth folded, next to the prepared pitcher and the glass.

7. Pour the liquid into the glass, making sure that the inside of the pitcher remains hidden from view.

8. Put the pitcher down just to the left of the glass. Pick up the prepared cloth, open it and turn it to show both sides.

9. Lay the cloth over the glass so that the cardboard disc (known to magicians as a "form") lies perfectly on top of the glass.

10. Lift the glass from above with your right hand and move it to your left. Note how the cloth passes directly over the jug. As it does, secretly drop the glass inside the jug and carry on moving to your left. The form will hold the shape of the glass beneath the cloth. Hold it between the right fingers and thumb.

11. You should now be moving away from the table and to the front of the stage. Count to three and toss the cloth into the air. The "vanish" is startling.

12. Catch the cloth and show it on both sides before putting it away and continuing with your show.

Going into Liquidation

A glass of liquid vanishes, reappearing inside a box that was previously shown to be empty. This trick was originally performed using a spectator's hat, but the box makes a good substitute. This trick uses the same gimmicked cloth as the Vanishing Glass of Liquid.

1. Set the folded, gimmicked cloth inside a small box and have a glass of liquid nearby.

2. Show the glass of liquid to the spectators then cover it with your special cloth.

3. Pick up the box and show that it is empty.

> ## TIP
> Because of the similarity of this trick with the Vanishing Glass of Liquid you will not want to have both in the same show. However, when you are learning it is interesting to see how the same effect can be achieved using a variety of methods. Knowing more than one way to make something happen allows you to choose the best method for any given show.

4. Say that the glass is going to fly to the box. As you say this, mimic the flight of the glass, holding it from above, and place the covered glass inside the box.

5. Leave the glass inside, removing only the cloth, which will maintain the shape of the glass. Move away and prepare to throw the glass up into the air.

6. Throw the cloth high above you, making the glass of liquid vanish.

7. Catch the cloth and show both sides to the audience.

8. Finally, reveal to your audience that the glass of liquid really is in the box as you promised it would be.

Liquidated Assets

Liquid is poured into an empty cardboard box, which magically remains totally dry. Like Going into Liquidation, this routine originally used a borrowed hat. It is very effective, and it uses cheap and easy-to-make props.

1. Construct a simple gimmick by cutting the rim off a plastic cup.

2. Now cut the base out of a second plastic cup.

3. When these two cups are nested together they look like one.

4. Have your special cup and a pitcher of liquid on one table and the box on the other. Hold the cup and show that the box is empty and dry.

5. Explain to the spectators that there is an old trick in which the magician pours water into a cardboard box without damaging it. The secret, you go on to explain, is to sneak an empty cup into the box when no one is looking. Show the cup empty and put it into the box.

Secret View

6. Now explain that you are going to do the trick without the cup! Reach into the box and remove the bottomless cup only (the inner cup). Make sure you do not "flash" the bottom of the cup to the spectators.

7. Pour some liquid from the pitcher, apparently into the box, but actually into the hidden cup. Suitable expressions help to sell the idea that the liquid is sloshing around the bottom of the box.

Secret View

8. Take the cup and say you'll perform some magic. Put the cup into the box. In doing so, nest it inside the other one, which is now full of liquid.

9. Take the filled cup from the box and pour the liquid back into the pitcher with a flourish.

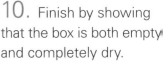

10. Finish by showing that the box is both empty and completely dry.

Multiplication Sensation

The last six digits of the number on a credit card are read out loud and multiplied by a number chosen by a spectator. The magician shows a prediction, which was made before the show started. It matches the total exactly.

1. You will need a slip of paper, a marker, a calculator, a pair of scissors, and some tape.

2. Write the number 142857 on the paper. Be sure to leave a small space between each digit.

3. Now carefully tape the edges of the paper together so that the digits are on the outside of the loop. Use a pair of scissors to cut the tape neatly and apply it to the back of the paper only, so that the connection is invisible.

4. In performance, display your prediction at your fingertips. No one should be able to see that the paper is one continuous loop of numbers. Place the prediction to one side or in a pocket.

5. Now take a credit card from your wallet and explain that you will read the last six digits of the number. Pretend to read from the card, but instead call out the number 142857. Ask a spectator to enter this number into a calculator.

6. Ask your helper with the calculator to multiply the number by any whole number from 1 to 6. The secret is that no matter which number they multiply by, the answer will consist of the same six digits but in a different, cyclical order. It will be 285714, 428571, 571428, 714285, or 857142.

Secret View

7. Once the answer is read out loud, secretly and quickly tear the paper between the appropriate numbers.

8. Display your prediction, which will match the total on the calculator.

Square Circle Production

For this trick you need to make a clever prop that has endless uses. It is an ideal way to make something appear – anything that will fit inside the box. It has been used by magicians for generations and is incredibly deceptive. Its great advantage is that, unlike many other production boxes, you can use this one when surrounded by spectators. The illusion is so versatile that you can even make a giant one from which you can produce a person. You can also buy professional square circle production boxes from many magic shops.

1. You will need several sheets of cardboard in different colors, tape or glue, a pair of scissors or a craft knife, and some black paint. First, make a tube from a sheet of black cardboard.

2. Now make a larger tube from a sheet of blue cardboard: it needs to slip easily over the black tube and to be about 1 in (2.5 cm) taller.

3. You now need to construct a square tube that is the same height as the black tube and that will fit easily around the blue tube. Cut some slots out of the front panel of the box so the spectators will be able to see inside it.

4. This square tube should be painted black inside.

5. These are the separate pieces you should have: a square tube painted black inside, a blue tube that fits inside it, and a black tube that fits inside the blue one and is a little shorter.

6. Set up the trick by placing the blue tube over the black tube and the red tube over everything. Place the box on a table. The surface should be black, so you will need a black tablecloth or a mat large enough to set your square circle production on. Put whatever you wish to produce by magic inside the black tube.

7. To begin, pick up the red tube and move it around to show the spectators that it is empty. Replace it in position around the blue tube.

8. Now pick up the blue tube and once again show that it is empty by pushing your arm through it. While you are doing this you can see that the black inner tube is invisible, as it looks like the inside of the red tube. This principle is called "black art" and is used in numerous magic tricks. When it is used properly no one should ever know there is anything there.

9. Replace the blue tube between the red one and the black one, say the magic words, and then lift all three tubes together to reveal the item.

Mini Flip-Flap Production Box

This small box can be shown empty and then used to produce anything that will fit inside it. In the next chapter you will see how a larger version of the box can be used to make a person appear. If you are good at craft projects, you can make this box out of wood.

1. You will need some double-walled corrugated cardboard to make the box. Cut a rectangular panel as shown, approximately 6 x 12 in (15 x 30 cm), and fold it in the middle. Cut the center out of one side: this will be the top of the box.

2. Now cut a second, identically sized panel and fold as before.

3. Tape the two panels together to make a box that will hinge flat.

4. Cut two 6 in (15 cm) square doors that fit the open sides of the box perfectly.

5. Make a second, smaller box approximately 2 x 2 x 3 in (5 x 5 x 7.5 cm) and glue it to one of the doors.

6. Attach the doors to the front and back of the box using adhesive tape, so that they flip open in opposite directions. The small box should be inside the main box when the door is closed.

7. Load the small box with the items you are going to produce. In this case you'll use silk handkerchiefs. The ends are twisted together in order to make them easier to remove during the trick.

Secret View

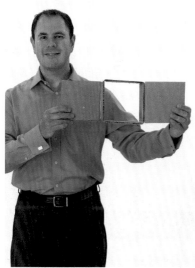

8. To begin the performance hold the box up with the loaded section on the back of the front door.

9. Open the box by moving your left hand to the left while your right hand stays where it is. This ensures that the loaded box is always shielded from view behind the door.

10. This is the view from the front. It looks as if you are showing a completely empty box.

Secret View

11. From the back the box now looks like this.

12. Continue to move the box all the way around, always keeping your right hand still so the box pivots around the loaded door.

13. Grip all the sections with your right hand to flatten the box, proving that it is empty.

14. From the front, it looks as if it would be impossible to hide anything inside the box.

15. Reverse the moves to reassemble the box. Now make a magical gesture.

16. Reach into the hole in the top of the box, and start to produce the silk handkerchiefs one at a time.

17. Of course you can use any object that will fit into the inner box.

18. If you wish, you can replace the silks in the box to finish the trick.

19. Open the doors to show the silks have vanished again. So this is not just a production box but a vanishing box, too.

20. Don't forget to flatten the box, as this will make the vanishing effect even more convincing.

Silk Through Glass (version 1)

A silk handkerchief penetrates the bottom of a glass. This is one of a variety of methods for performing this trick, and it is very effective. Try practicing in front of a mirror so that you make appropriate facial gestures, and work on your patter before you perform.

1. You should use the thinnest, most invisible thread you can find for this. Fishing line works very well. Prepare a silk handkerchief by attaching a short length of thread to one corner. This thread should be knotted at the end.

2. Display the silk in one hand (with the thread hidden in your hand) and a glass in the other.

3. Insert the handkerchief into the glass, allowing the thread to secretly trail out of the glass.

Secret View

4. This secret view shows how the thread should be positioned.

5. Show a second silk handkerchief in the other hand.

6. Place this on top of the first silk in the glass. Pick up a larger handkerchief.

7. Place the large handkerchief over the whole glass. Secure it with a rubber band around the mouth of the glass.

8. Lift up the large handkerchief to show the silks inside the glass.

Secret View

9. Reach underneath and feel for the trailing thread. Begin to pull down on the thread.

10. The bottom silk will be pulled out of the sealed glass, under the band and down toward your hand. Grip the corner of the silk, and continue to pull it down. It will appear to be penetrating the bottom of the glass.

11. Lift the handkerchief to show the other silk still in position in the top of the glass.

12. Finally, remove the large handkerchief and the rubber band.

Silk Through Glass (version 2)

This is a variation of the method used for the previous trick. This version uses no gimmicks at all. It can be performed totally impromptu, as you should be able to find a glass and a few handkerchiefs or napkins in most places.

1. Display a silk handkerchief in one hand and a glass in the other.

2. Insert the silk into the glass and prepare to cover everything with a larger, opaque handkerchief

Secret View

3. As soon as the glass is hidden out of sight, secretly allow it to swivel upside down.

4. Wrap a band around the base of the glass. (Your audience will assume it is the top of the glass.)

5. It is now easy to pull the silk down, creating the illusion that it is penetrating the base of the glass.

6. Pull the band and the handkerchief off the glass.

Secret View

7. At the same time turn the glass back to the upright position while it is still concealed by the handkerchief.

8. You can finish by handing out everything for examination, if you wish.

Switching Bag

This clever bag can be used to switch objects, make things appear and even make them disappear. The bag is extremely simple to make, and if you wish to make a more professional looking, longer lasting bag, you can stitch rather than glue the material together.

1. Make the bag from felt. Start by cutting out a rectangle approximately 10 x 12 in (25 x 30 cm) and a smaller piece just a little less than 10 in (25 cm) square. Apply glue to the areas shaded in black.

2. Fold the rectangle in half, with the smaller square sandwiched in between. Make sure the pieces are securely glued so the bag won't fall apart during tricks.

3. You now have a bag with two sections. The central piece of fabric should be a fraction shorter than the two sides, so that it cannot be seen.

4. To hide the central section turn the top 1 in (2.5 cm) of fabric inside out to create a "cuff" around the edge. This completes the bag.

Blended Silks (version 2)

Four separate silks are placed in the empty bag. They come out joined together as one blended square. Some magic shops stock "Blendo" silks, which are made up of a mixture of colors specifically for tricks like this one. They are a good investment.

1. Using double-sided tape carefully join together four silks, in four different colors, along the edges to make one large square.

2. Put this blended silk into one side of your switching bag.

3. Turn over the cuff so that the empty side is open.

4. Display four separate silks, matching the four silks in the blended square, in a glass.

5. Turn the bag inside out to show the audience that it is empty.

6. Now place the separate silks in the bag's empty compartment one at a time.

7. When the silks are all inside the bag, make a magical gesture.

Secret View

8. At the same time as you open the bag, switch compartments.

9. Reach into the secret compartment to pull out the blended silk.

10. Hold up the silk by the edges, and wait for the applause!

Candy Caper

This is my favorite use for the switching bag. A glass of confetti is poured into the bag. A magic word is said, and the confetti changes into colorful candy that you can share with your audience. This trick is perfect for a children's show.

1. Prepare the switching bag by filling the secret compartment with small candies. Fill a glass with paper confetti, and have it on your table. Show the audience that your bag is empty.

2. Let the colorful confetti fall from a height into the empty side of your bag.

3. Give the bag a shake, and simultaneously switch the sides.

4. Pour out the candy from a modest height so that everyone can hear it hitting the sides of the glass.

5. There's only one thing left to do: Offer the candy to your audience, and help them eat it.

Escapologist

Despite your hands being tied together with a handkerchief, you are able to escape from a rope that secures you. This is a great trick, but you must practice it a lot if you are to make it deceptive.

1. Ask a spectator to tie your wrists together with a handkerchief or silk.

2. Now ask them to thread a length of rope between your arms.

3. They hold on to the ends and pull to confirm that you cannot escape.

Secret View

4. Just before they pull, you must work a little piece of the rope between the heels of your palms, as shown.

5. Move your hands to the left and right to show you can't escape, but as you move, work the rope further into your hands.

Secret View

6. This is clearly shown in this close-up view.

7. The movement of your arms hides the fact that you are now slipping the rope over your left hand.

Secret View

8. Again, this close-up shows exactly what is happening.

Secret View

9. Once the rope is over your hand, pull back sharply: The rope will work its way under the handkerchief on the side of your hand.

10. You will be released from the rope, but you can show that your wrists are still genuinely tied together.

Lord of the Rings

A solid ring links on to a length of rope, whose ends are firmly tied to your wrists. Here, the ring was made of rope, but you can use a bangle or any other object that fits over your wrist. Avoid performing both this trick and Escapologist in the same show.

1. You will need two identical rings and a length of rope.

Secret View

2. Prepare by placing one of the rings over your wrist and hiding it up your right sleeve.

3. In performance, have someone tie one end of the rope around each of your wrists. Show the ring, and explain that you will get it onto the rope. Of course, this sounds impossible.

4. Ask someone to cover your hands with a large cloth.

Secret View

5. Under cover of the cloth (removed here for clarity) secretly hide the loose ring inside your shirt.

7. Remove the cloth to show you have caused one solid object to penetrate another.

Secret View

6. Pull the duplicate ring out of your sleeve, over your wrist, and onto the length of rope.

Magic Circles

One of the most famous magic tricks of all time is called linking rings. In this simplified version, loops of cloth magically double in size and join together. Use plain woven cotton that will tear easily along the weave – a strip from an old bed sheet would be ideal. This is very cost-effective, as you will be able to make up several sets of loops from just one sheet.

1. You will need a strip of cotton 4 in (10 cm) wide and 5 ft (1.5 m) long. Prepare it by making a cut approximately 4 in (10 cm) deep in the middle of one end. Repeat this at the other end.

2. Apply strips of double-sided adhesive tape along the edge at one end.

3. Twist the right-hand side of the strip about 180 degrees (a half twist) before joining it neatly to the opposite end of the strip.

4. Twist the left-hand section 360 degrees (a full twist) before joining it to the opposite end.

5. Finish the preparation by making 3 in (7.5 cm) slits through the center of the divided sections on each side.

6. In performance show the loop of cloth, hiding the prepared section in your hand.

7. Tear the loop exactly in two by pulling the two halves apart, starting at the divided section.

8. This is the view as seen from the front.

9. When you have torn the strips, the result will be two separate loops, one in each hand.

10. Place the fully twisted loop over your shoulder and tear the half-twisted hoop into two again. Your tear should start from the slit you prepared earlier.

11. This will result in a giant loop, twice the size of the original.

TIP

If you prepare two cloth loops, one regular loop and one with your special twists, you can invite a spectator to copy every move you make. While they keep halving the size of their loops, you can link and grow yours.

12. Tear the remaining, fully twisted loop in half.

13. Two loops will form, one linked to the other.

Crazy Spots!

A normal, flat piece of card stock is shown to have four sides! This clever trick also has a great surprise ending. It is called a "sucker effect," as your audience thinks you are explaining how the trick works, and then you surprise them with a twist at the end.

1. To prepare the trick you need to begin with three sheets of black card stock, all identical in size: about 8 x 6 in (20 x 15 cm) is perfect.

2. Fold two of the pieces of card stock in half, and glue them together as shown.

3. Glue this T-shaped piece onto the third sheet of card stock to create a flap that can be positioned up or down.

4. Cut out 15 circles from a sheet of white paper. These will be the domino spots.

5. Glue two spots onto one side of the flap, as shown.

6. Fold the flap over, and glue eight spots on this section.

7. Place a tiny piece of double-sided tape at the top of this side. When you fold up this flap, it will be held shut by the tape.

8. Turn the whole thing over, and glue five spots on this side, as shown.

9. To perform the trick, start by holding the "domino" in your right hand so that your fingers cover the blank space. It will look as though you have six spots on view.

10. Bring your left hand up to the card from behind, to cover the blank space at the bottom of that side.

11. Turn the card with your left hand to show "three" spots on that side.

12. Grip the domino with your right hand so that your hand hides the center spot on the reverse side.

13. Turn the card to show "four" spots.

14. Your left hand hides the bottom spot on the other side and once again turns the card.

15. This time only one spot can be seen.

16. Now you explain to your audience how the trick works by showing how three spots or one spot can be seen depending on where you place your hands.

Secret View

17. Turn the card over, and repeat the explanation for six spots or four. At the same time, secretly detach the tape from the flap and carefully flip the secret flap down.

18. All this should remain unseen by your spectators, who are looking at the front of the card.

19. As you finish your explanation, turn the card over to reveal eight spots all over it!

Parade of Colors

Although you try to sort small balls into their different colors, they seem to get jumbled up in the most bizarre fashion. This is quite a long trick to remember, but lots of practice will ensure a smooth and baffling performance. Patter will help to keep spectators entranced.

1. You will need three colored boxes and three small balls of each color. Rolled-up tissue paper works perfectly. Set out the props as shown here.

2. Pick up the blue ball in the fingertips of your right hand, and prepare to drop it inside the blue box.

Secret View

3. As your hand goes into the box and out of sight, secretly position the ball behind your fingers and remove your hand.

4. With the blue ball still secretly palmed, pick up the orange ball and prepare to place it in the orange box.

Secret View

5. As your hand goes into the box, switch balls and drop the blue ball inside.

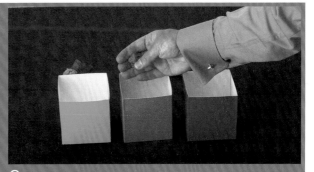

6. The orange ball now remains hidden in your hand as you lift your hand up.

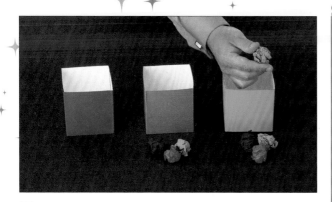

7. Pick up the green ball and supposedly drop that inside the green box.

8. In fact, you switch balls once again, and drop the orange ball, keeping the green one secretly in your hand.

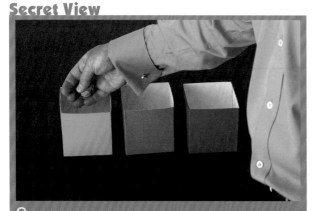

9. Remove your hand, secretly holding the green ball. Start the sequence again. First, pick up the blue ball and put it in the blue box, switching it for the green ball. Then pick up the orange ball and actually drop it in. Now pick up the green ball, and switch it for the blue ball in your hand. The final time, you pick up the blue ball and actually place it in the blue box; pick up the orange ball and switch it for the green ball as it goes into the orange box; and finally, pick up the green ball and actually put it in the green box.

10. The right hand still secretly holds an orange ball. Add this to the blue box as you tip the outer boxes upside down and let the contents fall out.

11. Finally, tip the balls out of the center box. The balls should all match their boxes, but it seems the colors have mixed themselves up again.

Paper Balls Over the Head

Three paper balls vanish one at a time in the most impossible way. This trick was made famous by one of magic's greatest exponents, Tony Slydini. He was a master of misdirection, and in his hands this one magic trick could entertain the biggest audiences. The trick can be done with all sorts of objects, but it needs careful practice and rehearsal with a friend. It is a strange routine in that the only person fooled by the trick is the volunteer who is on stage with you. Your whole audience will see how this trick is done.

1. Invite a spectator on to the stage and sit her sideways to the audience. Give her a paper ball to hold in each hand, and hold a third in the fingertips of your right hand.

2. Explain that you are going to put the paper ball into your left hand and that it will disappear on the count of three. Actually place the ball in your left hand as you speak. Take it back into your right hand and start the count.

3. Each time you count out loud, raise your right hand just above the volunteer's eyeline. On "three," gently toss the ball over her head as your hand moves up.

4. Immediately pretend to place the ball in your left hand and close it as if it contains the ball. If you have succeeded, your volunteer will not have seen the ball tossed over her head and will believe it is in your left hand.

5. Open both hands to show they are empty.

6. Repeat the sequence with one of the balls the volunteer is holding.

7. Do it one final time. Each time it seems to be more impossible than the last time.

8. The volunteer will be amazed.

Incredible Prediction

Three colored cards are shown, and a spectator is asked to choose one. You prove that you knew beyond a doubt which color they would opt for. It is based on the principle known among magicians as a "multiple out," as the trick can end in a number of different ways. It has been applied to thousands of tricks and is extremely effective and supremely baffling. Of course you must never perform this trick again to the same audience as they will be aware of the various outcomes and will work out how the trick is done.

1. You will need an envelope and some sheets of colored card stock: two orange, two blue, and one yellow. Prepare the envelope by sticking one orange card to the back.

2. Put a large "X" on the back of the yellow card.

3. Insert the two blue cards, one yellow card (with the "X" on the back), and one orange card into the envelope.

4. Draw a large question mark on the front of the envelope, and explain to your audience that you are about to prove that you can accurately predict a future event.

5. Reach into the envelope and remove three cards (orange, blue, and yellow), leaving the duplicate blue card secretly inside.

6. Keep the envelope in view, being careful not to flash the orange card on the back of it. Fan out the three colors and ask a spectator to choose which color she wants. Make sure you give her a chance to change her mind.

7. If the spectator chooses blue, ask someone to reach inside the envelope and remove the contents. It will be a blue card and you will have proved you knew what the choice would be. (Again, be careful not to flash the orange card on the back of the envelope.)

8. If orange is the spectator's choice, turn the envelope around to reveal your prediction on the back.

9. Finally, if yellow was chosen, turn all the cards around and show the large "X" on the back of the yellow card, again proving you knew which one it would be.

Vanishing Mug of Liquid

A mug filled with liquid is turned upside down on a spectator's head. The liquid disappears, leaving the mug empty. Be careful not to show the inside of the mug when you do this trick, and make sure your helper receives a round of applause for being such a great sport.

1. Cut out the absorbent section of a disposable diaper. This contains crystals that are able to absorb many times their own weight in liquid.

2. Add some double-sided adhesive tape to the underside of the diaper and stick it inside a mug with a white interior. The diaper will be a tight fit, so you will need to pack it in.

3. Set the prepared mug and a pitcher of liquid on a table with a sheet of card stock. Invite a spectator to join you on stage and sit them down next to you.

4. Slowly pour about half a mugful of liquid into the mug. The diaper will absorb everything.

5. Explain to everyone that you are going to demonstrate a science experiment with some liquid and some cardboard.

6. Lay the piece of card stock on top of the mug of liquid.

7. Turn everything upside down, using a quick but smooth action.

8. Place the mug and the card on your volunteer's head.

9. Slip out the card, but then admit that you've forgotten exactly how the experiment works!

10. However, since you're a magician, it is easy to make the liquid disappear. Simply say some magic words, and slowly lift the mug up into the air. The liquid will have vanished.

Incredible Blindfold Act

This routine is really offered for laughs rather than as a serious mind-reading illusion. Even so, right until the end your audience will wonder how your assistant is able to tell which objects are being held up in the air while they are blindfolded. When you ask your assistant what you are holding, he or she should not just say, "You are holding a watch," but something like, "I am getting the sense of movement, a sweeping motion, yes, of something moving but very small movements. In fact, I see time passing slowly. Yes, the movement I see is a hand on a watch. This is a watch." Building it up like this adds a believability factor to the magic trick, which only makes it funnier when the spectators see how it was done. The success of the trick depends on how good your assistant's acting skills are.

1. Your assistant is seated sideways to the audience and blindfolded with a thick black cloth.

2. Objects are borrowed from various members of the audience and held up in the air in front of the assistant. Despite being blindfolded, the assistant is able to explain which objects have been chosen.

3. When you stand and take a bow with your assistant at the end, everyone laughs as they see a big hole in the side of the blindfold that was hidden until this point.

Watch This!

A watch disappears, only to reappear on your wrist moments later. The cloth used in this trick is known as a "Devil's handkerchief." It can be used to make lots of things disappear in a very convincing fashion and is used by professional magicians.

1. Make a double cloth by stitching two identical cloths together around the edges, leaving half of one edge open.

2. Prepare for the trick by placing two identical watches on your wrist. One should be hidden up your sleeve and the other should be visible.

3. Position the cloth over your shoulder so that your fingers can immediately grasp the unstitched section.

4. When you start to perform the trick, remove the visible watch.

5. As you pull your sleeve down, secretly pull the other watch farther down your arm to your wrist. No one will notice this.

6. Pull the cloth off your shoulder with your left hand, making sure that you grip the open section. Hold the cloth open to display it. The watch is held between the fingers of your right hand.

7. Gather up the corners of the cloth to form a little bag.

8. Drop the watch into the secret pocket. It looks just as if it is dropping into the folds of the cloth.

9. Drop all the corners except for the one in your left hand (which is the prepared corner).

10. Show the cloth, back and front. The watch is safely and totally hidden in between the two layers.

11. Finally, drape the cloth over your right arm and pull back your left sleeve to show the watch back on your wrist.

Second Sight

A shuffled deck of cards is placed in a brown paper bag and held high above the magician's head. Despite the apparent fairness of the shuffling procedure, the cards are named one at a time before being removed from the bag. This is a very deceptive trick and is extremely baffling. You can also make an interesting presentation by pretending that you can see with your fingertips.

1. Cut a small square out of the bottom right corner of a brown paper bag.

2. When the bag is folded flat, the hole is hidden perfectly.

3. You can open the bag and show that it is empty. Just put your finger over the hole and keep the bag moving. No one will notice the tiny piece missing.

4. Have a deck of cards thoroughly shuffled, and then clearly place them inside the paper bag.

5. Hold the bag up high over your head, and explain that you will be using a technique called "second sight" to establish which card you are going to pull out.

Secret View

6. As you reach into the bag, glimpse the bottom card of the deck through the hole. This is the card you will remove.

7. Call out the name of the card, and then remove it from the bag in order to show your audience you are correct. Repeat this as many times as you wish, each time naming a card before removing it.

Excalibur's Cup

A plastic cup is placed on top of a book and a child is asked to lift it. They do, without a problem. You place a silk handkerchief in the cup and explain that you will hypnotize an adult into believing that the silk weighs a ton, and they will be unable to lift the cup. Unbelievably, they can't! You can enhance the presentation by creating a story that provides a reason or "plot" for the effect.

1.Cut a small hole, big enough for you to fit your thumb through, in the bottom of a plastic cup, as shown.

2.Set the cup on a book with the hole hidden at the rear, and ask a child to lift up the cup. They do. Ask them to replace it.

Secret View

3. Insert your thumb into the hole, and secretly pin the cup to the book. Show a silk, and place it inside the cup.

4.Now ask someone else to raise the cup off the book. They will be unable to do so.

Anti-Gravity Glasses

Two ordinary glasses, which can be examined by the spectators, are placed on a book but don't fall off when it is turned upside down, apparently defying gravity. This is a very old trick, which has baffled audiences for many years.

1. You will need two plastic tumblers, two beads, some fine thread, a handkerchief, two silks, a pair of scissors, and a hardback book.

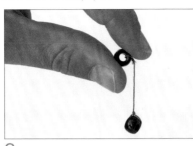

2. To prepare the trick, tie the two beads together with thread, leaving a length of approximately 1 in (2.5 cm) between them. (This length may need adjusting to suit the size of your hand.)

3. Make a small slit in the hem of a handkerchief, or open a little of the stitching, and insert the two beads. Work them down to the middle of one of the edges.

4. To perform, show the tumblers to the spectators, and then insert a silk into each one. Show the handkerchief; then lay it flat on the table. The beads should be at the edge opposite you. Place a hard-back book horizontally in the center of the handkerchief on the table.

5. Fold the left side of the hand-kerchief neatly over the edge of the book, as shown here.

6. Now fold the other side of the handkerchief over the edge of the book, too.

7. Bring the side of the handker-chief nearest to you up over the edge of the book.

8. Finally, the side with the beads should be folded over.

9. Pick up the book, gripping it and the handkerchief as shown. Place your thumb directly between the two beads.

10. Take one of the plastic tumblers with a silk inside.

11. Turn it upside down, and position it on the book so that the rim goes over one of the beads and rests against your thumb. Notice how a small corner of silk is protruding from the tumbler. Repeat with the second tumbler.

12. Turn everything upside down, supporting the tumblers with your other hand, but then let go.

13. The tumblers are pinned in place between the beads and your thumbs so they will remain suspended.

14. Slowly pull out one of the colored silks to prove the tumblers are not connected to the book.

15. Repeat the action, and remove the other silk.

16. Pause for a moment to add drama to the performance.

17. Turn the book over, and remove the tumblers one at a time.

18. Unwrap the book. Everything apart from the handkerchief can be examined.

Common Optical Illusions

There are many different types of optical illusions, some of which occur naturally, and others that have been created. Certain optical illusions trick the brain into believing that objects are smaller or larger than another object of the same size. Others are images that can be viewed in more than one way. They all distort our ability to apply rational thinking to a given problem.

Which Is Longer?

Although the top line appears to be shorter than the bottom line, they are in fact the same length. This is called the Müller-Lyer illusion. It was first made famous in 1889.

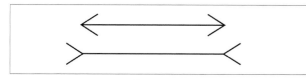

How Many Shelves?

Can you see three shelves or four shelves? How many you see depends on whether you look from the left or the right.

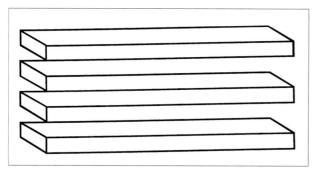

Shrinking Haze

If you stare at the spot in the middle of the gray haze, the haze will appear to shrink.

Small, Medium, Large

Take a look at these three images. Which do you think is the tallest – 1, 2, or 3? Actually they are all identical. The converging lines distort the images, and as the lines get closer together, the images seem to grow.

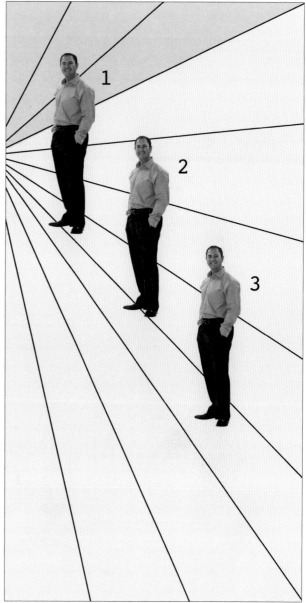

Connecting Line

In this rather odd optical illusion, it is difficult to work out which of the bottom two lines connects with the top line. Use a ruler or straight edge to check which line does join the top one.

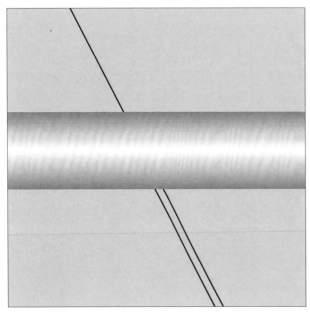

Full to the Brim

Is the hat below taller than it is wide? Or wider than it is tall? Both the width and the height are actually identical, although you probably won't believe it until you check with a ruler!

All Square

Have a look at the square below. Are the sides parallel? Are they perfectly straight or do the sides bend in? Believe it or not all of the sides are straight. The concentric circles appear to "pull" the lines inward, creating the illusion that the sides are curved.

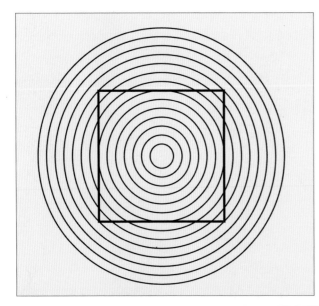

Odd Ball

This optical illusion is similar to All Square. The smaller circle looks as though it is not perfectly circular, although in reality it is. The rays emanating from the center distort the outline and make us perceive the circle as irregular.

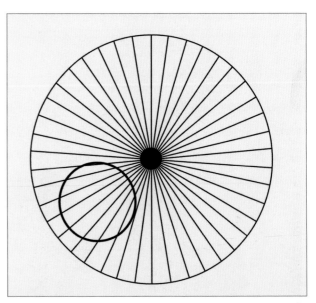

Straight or Crooked?

Take a look at the lines below. Even though they look like they converge in both directions, they are in fact absolutely parallel! Check with a ruler, if you like.

Scintillating Illusion

Look at this image for a couple of seconds. Do you see flickering black dots at the intersections of the squares? This effect, called scintillation, was first observed and reported in the early 19th century.

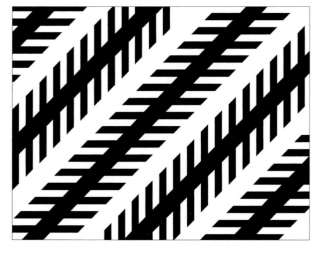

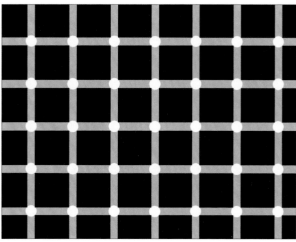

Parallel Lines

Are the horizontal lines parallel, or do they slope? They are actually absolutely parallel, but the offset squares create the optical illusion that the lines converge and, in some places, bulge. This effect is sometimes seen on tiled walls or floors.

Inuit or Warrior?

Take a look at this picture. What do you see?
Hint: The Native American warrior is facing the left; the Inuit is facing the right.

Young or Old Woman?

What do you see when you look at this famous optical illusion? Hint: The old woman's nose is the young woman's cheek.

Rabbit or Duck?

Which do you see, a rabbit or a duck? This famous illusion is thought to have been drawn by psychologist Joseph Jastrow in 1899.

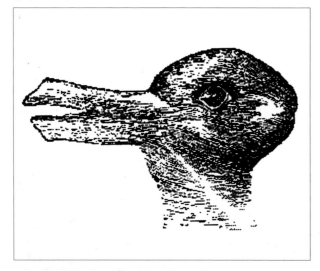

Toward or Away?

Is this open book facing toward you or away from you? There is no correct answer to this simple optical illusion.

Shrinking Pen

This fascinating optical illusion makes a pen or pencil shrink in size before your eyes. Watch yourself in the mirror, and you will see how good it looks. The illusion is best when it is viewed from the front. This is a quick and easy illusion that can easily be incorporated into a magic show or simply demonstrated at a party. It works best if the pen is a different color from the top that you are wearing.

1. Hold a pen in your left finger-tips so that your left hand covers just under one-third of the pen when viewed from the front.

2. Now transfer the pen to the fingertips of the right hand.

3. The right hand's grip is identical to the left hand's grip. If these movements are repeated at a speed of about four transfers per second, the pen seems to shrink when viewed from the front.

Floating Sausage

This popular illusion is an example of a stereogram. This effect occurs when two images, one from each of your eyes, are incorrectly combined in your brain, causing them to overlap and – in this case – create a third finger floating between the two real fingers.

Hold the tips of your first fingers about ½ in (1 cm) apart and about 8 in (20 cm) from your eyes. Now stare at your fingers and bring them slowly toward the tip of your nose. You will see a sausage-like shape floating in the air between your fingers. There is, of course, nothing there. What you are seeing are the fingertips of each hand in reverse (as you are crossing your eyes). The result is a sausage shape where the two images overlap.

Hole in Hand

With a piece of paper or card, you can create an instant X-ray machine that enables you to see straight through your hand as if there were a hole in the middle of it.

Take a piece of paper or card stock and roll it into a tube. Hold the tube to your right eye with your right hand and keep both eyes open. Now hold up your left hand beside the tube with the palm toward you, and you'll see a hole appear in it! This is another example of a stereogram illusion, which occurs when your brain fuses two images, one from each eye, to create a single, combined image.

Ship in a Bottle

On one side of a piece of card draw a ship, on the other side draw a bottle. Simply by rotating the card, you can make it look as though the ship is inside the bottle. The images move so fast that they are retained for a fraction of a second in the mind's eye, thus merging together to become a single picture. You can try this illusion using other pictures, such as a bird in a cage, or maybe a goldfish in a bowl.

1. To create this optical illusion you will need a piece of card stock measuring 3 x 2 in (7.5 x 5 cm), a pen, a hole punch and two rubber bands.

2. Punch a hole centrally at each end of the card.

3. Push a rubber band through each hole, and loop one end through the other to attach them, as shown.

4. On one side of the card draw a big, empty bottle.

5. On the other side of the card, draw a ship. The images must be centered, and the ship must be small enough to fit inside the bottle. If you hold the card up to the light, you will be able to check that the positions are correct.

6. Hold a rubber band in each hand, and quickly twist the card back and forth. The spectator will see the ship appear inside the bottle.

◆ ◆ ◆ ◆ ◆ ◆ ◆

Emily's Illusion

I discovered this illusion while playing with one of my daughter's toys. It is a good example of how our eyes are slower to see than we think. Just like Ship in a Bottle, here the human eye sees two images and blurs them into one.

1. Draw thick parallel lines across the width of a piece of card stock. Hold it at your fingertips.

2. Throw the card up in the air, spinning it as fast as you can. Notice how the lines seem to be going in two directions. It seems that the card has a checked rather than a lined pattern on it.

Stretching Arm

As you pull your arm, it seems to stretch in the most peculiar way. Of course your arm is not actually stretching, but the effect is surprisingly effective. If you reverse the moves, you can also appear to make your arm shrink back to its normal length.

1. You need to be wearing a long-sleeved shirt for this illusion. Stand up, with your left side to the spectators, and then raise your left arm in front of you. Make sure that your elbow is slightly bent and that your sleeve is pulled right down to your wrist.

2. Pull your left wrist with your right hand and stretch your arm just a little. Your sleeve will stay where it is, but your arm will move forward.

3. Repeat this movement in short bursts, moving your left shoulder forward slightly as you do so.

Pinkie Down

The little finger of your left hand shrinks until it is tiny. The more slowly you perform this illusion, the more amazing it is. American magician Meir Yedid performs a whole act in which each of his fingers appears to shrink and then disappear, one by one.

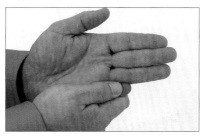

1. Hold your left hand out flat, palm facing the spectators.

Secret View

4. This is an exposed view of how your hand looks from beneath.

2. Grip your little finger with your right thumb covering all but the last ¼ in (6 mm) at its tip. Wrap the fingers of your right hand around the back of your left hand.

3. Slide your right hand back and as you do, so bend the little finger at the joint, but ensure that its pad stays in line with the rest of your left hand. Keep sliding the thumb back until you can go no farther. It will look as if your little finger is shrinking. Reverse the action to stretch it back to normal size.

Thumb Stretch

You hold the tip of your thumb in your teeth and stretch it until it is more than twice as long as it was before! All the moves happen very fast, and the stretched thumb is seen for only about half a second. Of course, the illusion must only be viewed from the front.

Secret View

1. Hold your left thumb to your mouth, and lightly bite the very tip of it.

2. Bring your right hand up and insert the tip of the right thumb in your mouth, exchanging thumb tips. Reposition your left thumb inside your right fist.

3. Now stretch out your right thumb (with a groan of pain), and simultaneously pull your left thumb out of your right fist, creating the illusion that it has stretched.

4. From the side you can see what is really happening. Now reverse the moves and finish in the same position you started in.

◆ ◆ ◆ ◆ ◆ ◆ ◆

Thumb Off

You apparently unscrew the top of your thumb, and then screw it back on. This is one of the oldest and most popular tricks in existence, and you may have seen it done before. However, few people do it properly. When done well, it is an amazing optical illusion.

Secret View

1. Form a circle with the thumb and index finger of your right hand, and insert your left thumb into the hole.

2. Twist your left hand back and forth, explaining to the audience that you are unscrewing your thumb.

3. With a quick shake of your hands adjust them by bending in your left and right thumbs. Then use your right forefinger to cover the area where the thumbs meet. This is an exposed view.

4. From the front, the illusion is perfect. Wiggle the tip of your right thumb, which people will assume is still your left thumb.

5. Now slide your right hand along the side of your left forefinger. Slide it back again.

6. Finish with a quick shake of the hands to readjust them to the position in step 2, as you supposedly screw your thumb back on.

Impossible!

A piece of card is placed on the table. It has three cuts in it, yet the spectator cannot work out how the shape is formed from one piece of card alone. This is a very clever trick and is guaranteed to baffle most people the first time they try to work out how it is done.

1. Take a plain piece of card stock approximately 5 x 3 in (12.5 x 7.5 cm) and fold it in half lengthwise. With a pair of scissors, cut a slit from the middle of one edge to the central fold. Then turn the card around and cut two more slits on either side of the first slit from the opposite edge.

2. Holding the right half of the card steady, twist the left half 180 degrees.

3. Fold down the center section and you will have a very interesting optical puzzle: a shape that seems impossible to form from a single piece of card stock.

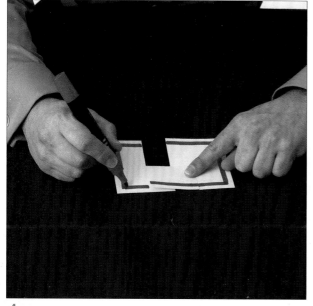

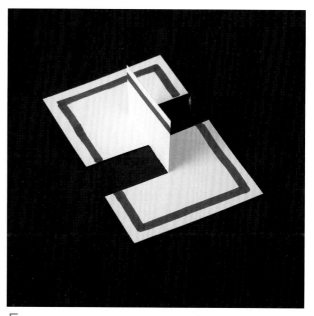

4. To add a really convincing touch, draw a border around the edge with a thick felt-tipped pen. Then fold over the center flap and draw the border across the gap, too.

5. This is how it should look when it is finished, and it is ready to try out on people.

Boomerang Cards

Two boomerang-shaped cards are displayed side by side, and it is clear that one is longer than the other. Yet, as you move them around, the cards seem to change size so that the smaller one becomes bigger and vice versa. Try it and discover for yourself how convincing it is.

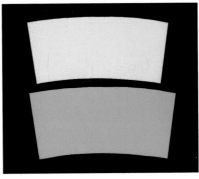

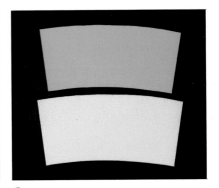

1. Cut out two cards of identical size and shape, as shown here. Use two different colors if you wish.

2. Place one card above the other, curving down. The card on the bottom will look bigger.

3. Pick up the top card, and move it to the bottom. Amazingly, it now looks as if it is the bigger one.

4. Try drawing a stick man on each card. The focus is then on the drawings rather than the cards themselves.

5. Switch the positions of the cards slowly and the illusion seems to happen right before your eyes!

Stamp It Out!

In this clever optical illusion, the principle known as refraction, or the bending of light, is responsible for making a stamp disappear from underneath a glass. Try it out with the props in front of you and you will appreciate just how clever and amazing this illusion is.

1. You will need a small pitcher of water, a glass (the taller the better), and a postage stamp. Place the stamp under the glass.

2. Slowly pour water into the glass until it is almost full. Watch the stamp and you will see it disappear.

3. If you look straight down into the glass from above you can still see the stamp, so if you want to stop people from doing this, place a plate on top of the glass after you have poured the water. It is now invisible from all angles.

TIP

If you want to make this into a magic trick, you can prepare the face of the stamp with double-sided tape so it adheres to the glass. In this way, you can lift the glass at the end, and the stamp really will be gone from the table!

East Meets West

The direction of an arrow drawn on a piece of paper can be changed without touching it, but how? Water bends light and refracts it in a weird and wonderful way. This experiment shows just how strange nature can sometimes be.

1. Fold a piece of card stock in half, and draw a large arrow on one side. Stand the card up on the table.

2. Place a glass in front of the card, and view the arrow through the glass.

3. To change the arrow's direction, simply pour some water into the glass.

Height of Failure

You ask someone to guess which is longer: the circumference of the mouth of a glass or the height of the glass. It is easier to understand how this optical illusion works if you imagine a football field: It's obvious that running all the way around the edge back to where you started is far longer than running straight down the field once. The same principle is at work here.

1. This illusion works best if you use a reasonably short glass with a wide mouth. Pose the question: "Which do you think is longer, the height of the glass or the circumference?" Most people will initially guess the height.

2. You can now raise the glass on objects such as boxes, books, playing cards, and wallets, until it is really high.

3. Add these things slowly, each time posing the question: "Now which do you think is longer?"

4. Each time you add something the spectators will probably still think that the height is longer, although the circumference is really still quite a bit longer.

5. You can prove this by winding string around the circumference and holding your finger to mark the length.

6. Then hold the string up against the glass to compare lengths.

Clip the Queen

As easy as it seems, spectators will not be able to put a paper clip on the queen card when you present it to them turned face down. Even when you know how the trick works, it is very difficult to put the paper clip on the correct card. This is an easy trick to prepare and is fun to keep in your bag ready for those occasions when someone asks you to do an impromptu trick.

1. Glue five old playing cards together in a fan. They should all be spot cards (ace–ten) except for the middle card, which should be a queen.

2. Hold the fan of cards face up, and ask someone to remember where the queen is. Give them a paper clip.

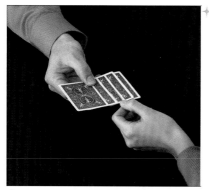

3. Turn the fan facedown, and ask them to put the paper clip on the card they think is the queen. It is most likely that they will put the paper clip on the center card.

4. When you turn the fan over again, you will see the paper clip is quite a distance away from the queen.

5. In order to find the queen, the paper clip needs to be in a position you just wouldn't expect, and people certainly won't think of it the first time they see this.

GLOSSARY

black art The use of a black background to help conceal or highlight objects in magic.

concentric Having a common center.

converge To incline toward each other, as lines that are not parallel.

gimmick An object that has been altered to help produce a magical effect, for example, by adding a secret box or a secret pocket.

impromptu Magic that can be performed on the spot using everyday items and without any special preparation.

mimic To imitate or copy.

misdirection Strategy used by a magician to control the focus of the spectator, for example, using a large movement to deflect attention from a smaller, secret movement.

opaque Not allowing light to pass through. An opaque material does not allow objects to be seen through it.

optical illusion A visually perceived image that uses color, light, and patterns to deceive or mislead the brain.

palm To hide an object in your hand.

patter Talk, such as stories or jokes, that accompanies a magician's performance.

penetrate To pass into or through.

production The appearance of an object or person, as if out of thin air, during a magic show.

prop Any item used in the performance of magic.

refraction The turning or bending of a light wave when it passes from one material (such as air) to another (such as water or glass).

silk A magician's handkerchief.

spectator A member of the audience.

stand-up magic A branch of magic in which the magician performs in front of a crowd.

stereogram An image or set of images that appears solid or three-dimensional.

summon To call forth; request to appear.

supernatural Being above or beyond what is natural or normal; appearing to violate the laws of nature.

Canadian Association of Magicians

Box 41
Elora, ON N0B 1S0
Canada
Web site: http://www.canadianassociationofmagicians.com
This organization promotes and encourages magicians and magic in Canada through magic conventions and other learning and networking opportunities. It is an official member of the FISM (International Federation of Magic Societies).

Exploratorium: The Museum of Science, Art, and Human Perception

Palace of Fine Arts
3601 Lyon Street
San Francisco, CA 94123
(415) 561-0362
Web site: http://www.exploratorium.edu
The Exploratorium is a museum with interactive science and art exhibits related to the topic of human perception. The SEEING collection includes both museum-based and online resources that explore how our eyes and brains construct the world we see. A wide range of visual phenomena is illustrated.

International Brotherhood of Magicians (IBM)

13 Point West Boulevard
St. Charles, MO 63301-4431
(636) 724-2400
Web site: http://www.magician.org
The International Brotherhood of Magicians (IBM) is a well-respected magic organization with over three hundred local rings, or chapters, worldwide. The organization welcomes amateur and professional magicians, magic collectors, and people with an interest in the art of magic. There are programs and resources designed especially for youth members.

Museum of Science, Boston

1 Science Park
Boston, MA 02114
(617) 723-2500
Web site: http://www.mos.org

The Museum of Science includes an exhibit called "Seeing Is Deceiving," which allows one to explore images that trick the eye and brain. The museum also offers live presentations that demonstrate the science in favorite magic tricks and optical illusions.

Museum of Vision

Foundation of the American Academy of Ophthalmology

655 Beach Street

San Francisco, CA 94109

(415) 561-8502

Web site: http://www.aaofoundation.org/what/heritage/index.cfm

This museum has fascinating resources to help the public understand the eye and visual system. The museum's publication Eye Openers: Exploring Optical Illusions *teaches the science behind optical illusions through demonstrations and activities.*

Society of American Magicians (SAM)

Society of Young Magicians (SYM)

P.O. Box 2900

Pahrump, NV 89041

(702) 610-1050

Web sites: http://www.magicsam.com; http://www.magicsym.com

Founded in 1902, the Society of American Magicians (SAM) is a worldwide organization dedicated to the art of magic. The Society of Young Magicians (SYM) is its youth branch, serving people ages 7–17 who are interested in learning and performing magic. SYM has about sixty local assemblies, or chapters, around the world, including in Canada, South Africa, and Bermuda.

Web Sites

Due to the changing nature of Internet links, Rosen Publishing has developed an online list of Web sites related to the subject of this book. This site is updated regularly. Please use this link to access the list:

http://www.rosenlinks.com/mag/stan

Barnhart, Norm. *Amazing Magic Tricks: Apprentice Level* (Edge Books: Magic Tricks). Mankato, MN: Capstone Press, 2009.

Becker, Helaine, and Claudia Dávila. *Magic Up Your Sleeve: Amazing Illusions, Tricks, and Science Facts You'll Never Believe.* Toronto, Canada: Maple Tree Press, 2010.

Burgess, Ron. *Kids Make Magic!: The Complete Guide to Becoming an Amazing Magician* (Quick Starts for Kids). Charlotte, VT: Williamson, 2004.

Davidson, Greg. *The Everything Magic Book: Everything You Need to Amaze, Baffle, and Entertain Your Friends* (Everything). Holbrook, MA: Adams Media Corp., 2000.

Diagram Group. *Visual Tricks* (A Little Giant Book). New York, NY: Sterling, 2007.

DiSpezio, Michael A. *Eye-Popping Optical Illusions.* New York, NY: Sterling, 2001.

DiSpezio, Michael A. *Optical Illusion Experiments* (No-Sweat Science). New York, NY: Sterling, 2007.

DK Publishing, Inc. *Magic and Illusion* (Cub Scout Activity Series). New York, NY: DK Publishing, 2007.

Eldin, Peter. *How to Be a Magician* (Most Excellent Book of—). North Mankato, MN: Stargazer Books, 2007.

Eldin, Peter. *Magic for Fun.* Brookfield, CT: Copper Beech Books, 2002.

Fullman, Joe. *The Great Big Book of Magic Tricks.* London, England: QED, 2009.

Kay, Keith. *Colorful Puzzles for Wise Eyes.* New York, NY: Sterling, 2007.

Kay, Keith. *Optical Illusions* (A Little Giant Book). New York, NY: Sterling; Lewes: GMC Distribution, 2007.

Keable-Elliott, Ian. *The Big Book of Magic Fun.* Hauppage, NY: Barrons Educational Series, Inc., 2005.

Kieve, Paul. *Hocus Pocus: A Tale of Magnificent Magicians.* New York, NY: Scholastic, 2008.

Longe, Bob. *The Jumbo Book of Magic Tricks.* New York, NY: Sterling, 2005.

Mason, Tom. *Disappearing Magic: How to Make Things Vanish Into Thin Air!* (Top Secret Magic). New York, NY: Scholastic, 2007.

Nurosi, Aki, and Mark Shulman. *Artful Illusions: Designs to Fool Your Eyes.* New York, NY: Sterling Juvenile; Poole: Chris Lloyd, 2006.

Seckel, Al. *Ambiguous Optical Illusions* (SuperVisions). New York, NY: Sterling, 2005.

Wick, Walter. *Walter Wick's Optical Tricks.* 10th anniversary ed. New York, NY: Scholastic, 2008.

Yoe, Craig. *The Mighty Big Book of Optical Illusions.* New York, NY: Price Stern Sloan, 2002.

INDEX

About the Author

Nicholas Einhorn is a Gold Star member of the Inner Magic Circle. He has won a number of industry awards for his work including: The Magic Circle Centenary Close-Up Magician 2005; F.I.S.M (World Magic Championships) Award Winner 2003; The Magic Circle Close-Up Magician of the Year 2002; and The Magic Circle Close-Up Magician of the Year 1996. Einhorn uses his magic to build crowds for some of the world's largest companies at business trade shows and exhibitions. He has many TV credits to his name and is regularly invited to lecture at magic societies and conventions around the globe. As a magic consultant, Einhorn has designed and created the special effects for several large-scale stage productions, as well as consulted on the film *Bright Young Things*, directed by Stephen Fry. He also develops and markets new magic effects for the magic fraternity. His illusions have been purchased and performed by magicians all over the world, including some of the biggest names in magic, such as Paul Daniels and David Copperfield.